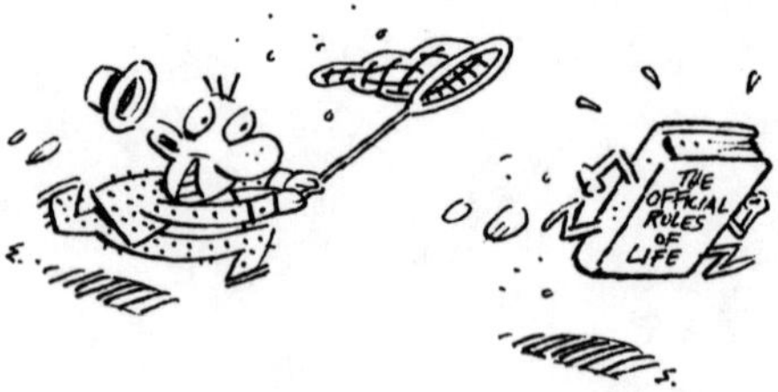
THE OFFICIAL RULES OF LIFE

THE
official rules
OF
life

. . . For Those of You Who Thought
You'd Mastered Life's Little
Instructions and Learned Everything
You Needed to Know

seth godin

A FIRESIDE BOOK   Published by Simon & Schuster
New York   London   Toronto   Sydney   Tokyo   Singapore

FIRESIDE
Rockefeller Center
1230 Avenue of the Americas
New York, NY 10020

Designed by Bonni Leon Berman
Illustrations by Elwood H. Smith

Manufactured in the United States of America

1   3   5   7   9   10   8   6   4   2

Library of Congress Cataloging-in-Publication Data
The official rules of life:–for those of you who thought you'd mastered life's little instructions and learned everything
you needed to know /[compiled by] Seth Godin.
p.   cm.
"A Fireside book."
1. Conduct of life–Quotations, maxims, etc. 2. Success–quotations, maxims, etc.   I. Godin, Seth.
BJ1581.2.O34   1996   95-46833
395–dc20   CIP
ISBN 0-684-80127-2

Contents

Introduction

Do murderers have rules? You betcha. Probably something like "Wear dark clothes. No bloody gloves." I'm making it up, but you get the picture. How about moving men? "Lift from the knees. Don't pack dirty dishes." Even an ant colony has rules. "Feed the big girl first."

What if you had a menu of rules from which to pick and choose the best bits of advice around? Custom-make your own credo! Write your own life handbook! Boss yourself around! Have a look at a handful of these *Official Rules of Life* and consider the possibilities.

From the New York Marathon Last Minute Tips there's: "Decide what to wear in advance." From baseball great Satchel Paige's Rules of Life, you choose: "Avoid fried meats which angry up the blood." And from the Miller Brewing Company, you agree you should: "Plan your drinking." All in all, it sounds like a recipe for a lifetime of successful late nights out.

Or this combination: "Don't look down." (from Anthony Robbins' Five Rules for Walking on Hot Coals); "Practice walking in all kinds of shoes." (from Arthur Elgort's *Models Manual*); and "Don't slouch!" (one of Superman's tips on attaining Super-

Health). Spend six months or so following those rules and you'll have the posture of a principal dancer with the Joffrey Ballet.

There's only one hitch. You have to be the kind of person who can do the rule thing. Face it. There are two sorts of people. There are those who see a rule, salute it, and snap right into line. And there are those who squint narrowly at a rule and immediately start figuring out a way around, over, or through the rule just because it's there. Oh, and there is a separate category of people who really represent rules in a concrete way. In a way, they *are* the rules. Cops, priests, referees. Like that.

What happens when one of these symbols of the rules (and usually the uniform gives him away) must submit to rules himself? Consider this snippet from the Official Major League Baseball Rules, specific to the regulation of umpires:

You are the only official representative of baseball on the ball field. It is often a trying position which requires the exercise of much patience and good judgment, but do not forget that the first essential in working out of a bad situation is to keep your own temper and self-control....Finally, be courteous, impartial and firm, and so compel respect from all.

Timothy Hurst, a loathed and feared umpire from another decade, had a little trouble with the rules. Hurst was known far and wide for settling arguments with players by punching them or spitting in their eyes. He was thrown out of the National League one year for throwing a beer stein at a fan and causing a bleacher-clearing brawl. Ten years later, at this point serving time in the American League, Hurst broke the temper and self-control rule one last time. Eddie Collins, the very popular second baseman for the Philadelphia Athletics, argued with one of Hurst's calls. "Get away from me or I'll spit in your eye," Hurst snarled. Collins didn't move and Hurst gobbed a lugar in Collins' eye. A stadium riot ensued and Hurst lost his job once and for all.

The moral of this story? Only get in bed with the rules you can keep. Look for rules the keeping of which promise to improve your lot. And don't, under any circumstances, spit in anyone's eye.

Alcoholics Anonymous:
The Twelve Steps

1. We admitted we were powerless over alcohol–that our lives had become unmanageable.

2. Came to believe that a power greater than ourselves could restore us to sanity.

3. Made a decision to turn our will and our lives over to the care of God as we understood Him.

4. Made a searching and fearless moral inventory of ourselves.

5. Admitted to God, ourselves and another human being the exact nature of our wrongs.

6. Were entirely ready to have God remove all these defects of character.

7. Humbly asked Him to remove our shortcomings.

8. Made a list of all persons we had harmed and became willing to make amends to them all.

9. Made direct amends to such persons wherever possible, except when to do so would injure them or others.

10. Continued to take personal inventory and, when we were wrong, promptly admitted it.

11. Sought through prayer and meditation to improve our conscious contact with God as we understood Him, praying only for knowledge of His will for us and the power to carry that out.

12. Having had a spiritual awakening as the result of these steps, we tried to carry this message to alcoholics and to practice these principles in all our affairs.

The American Kennel Club Guidelines
for Dog Show Judges

Excuse any dog that in your opinion:

- menaces

- threatens

- exhibits any sign that it may not be examined in the normal manner.

Disqualify any dog that in your opinion attacks any person in the ring.

Anthony Robbins' Five Rules for Walking on Hot Coals

1. Get and stay "in state."

2. Repeat your mantra: "Cool moss, cool moss."

3. Walk straight and normal.

4. Don't look down.

5. Wipe your feet on the other side.

Antioch University Sexual Offense Policy: Consent

All sexual contact and conduct on the Antioch College campus and/or occurring with an Antioch community member must be consensual.

1. For the purpose of this policy, "consent" shall be defined as follows: the act of willingly and verbally agreeing to engage in specific sexual contact or conduct.

2. If sexual contact and/or conduct is not mutually and simultaneously initiated, then the person who initiates sexual contact/conduct is responsible for getting the verbal consent of the other individual(s) involved.

3. Obtaining consent is an ongoing process in any sexual interaction. Verbal consent should be obtained with each new level of physical and/or sexual contact/conduct in any given interaction, regardless of who initiates it. Asking "Do you want to have sex with me?" is not enough. The request for consent must be specific to each act.

4. The person with whom sexual contact/conduct is initiated is responsible to express verbally and/or physically her/his willingness or lack of willingness when reasonably possible.

5. If someone has initially consented but then stops consenting during a sexual interaction, she/he should communicate withdrawal verbally and/or through physical resistance. The other individual(s) must stop immediately.

6. To knowingly take advantage of someone who is under the influence of alcohol, drugs, and/or prescribed medication is not acceptable behavior in the Antioch community.

7. If someone verbally agrees to engage in specific contact or conduct, but it is not of her/his own free will due to any of the circumstances stated in (a) through (d) below, then the person initiating shall be considered in violation of this policy if:

   a) the person submitting is under the influence of alcohol or other substances supplied to her/him by the person initiating;

b) the person submitting is incapacitated by alcohol, drugs, and/or pre-scribed medication;

c) the person submitting is asleep or unconscious;

d) the person initiating has forced, threatened, coerced, or intimidated the other individual(s) into engaging in sexual contact and/or sexual conduct.

Arthur Elgort's *Models Manual*

Save some money.

Don't bite your nails.

Don't complain.

Be on time.

Don't talk on the phone too long.

Practice walking in all kinds of shoes.

Look at yourself in the mirror once in a while.

Attaining Super-Health:
A Few Hints from Superman

The secret of building powerful muscular control is regular daily exercise! However **avoid overstrain!**

Don't weaken in your determination to exercise daily. It's hard work to stiffen soft muscles into **sinews of steel — but boy, it's worth it!**

In unity there is **strength!** Form **exercise clubs** with your close pals so that you'll all benefit!

Don't slouch! Keep your head high, shoulders back, chin in, and chest out. You'll be surprised at the confidence you gain in yourself.

A well-rounded diet is, of course, essential; fruits, vegetables, and plenty of milk are advisable.

Mental health is inextricably linked with physical health. Always do the right and just thing—Help others, keep your conscience clear . . . that's **super living!**

(circa 1938)

Avon's Principles

We will provide individuals an opportunity to develop and earn in support of their betterment and happiness.

We will serve families throughout the world with products of the highest quality, backed by a guarantee of satisfaction.

We will provide service to Representatives and Customers that is outstanding in its helpfulness and courtesy.

We will rely with full confidence on Associates and Representatives, recognizing that our corporate success depends on their individual contributions and achievements.

We will share with others the rewards of growth and success.

We will honor the responsibilities of corporate citizenship by contributing to the well-being of the society in which we function.

We will cherish and maintain the friendly spirit of Avon.

(circa 1898)

Baltasar Gracián's *Oraculo Manual*

Keep your affairs in suspense.

Make people depend on you.

Avoid victories over your superiors.

Control your imagination.

Know how to take and give hints.

Know how to be all things to all men.

Without lying, do not tell the whole truth.

Be a man without illusions.

Behave as if you were watched.

In a word, be a saint.

(circa 1650)

Boy Scout Laws

A Scout is **TRUSTWORTHY.** A Scout tells the truth. He keeps his promises. Honesty is a part of his code of conduct. People can always depend on him.

A Scout is **LOYAL.** A Scout is true to his family, friends, Scout leaders, school, nation, and world community.

A Scout is **HELPFUL.** A Scout is concerned about other people. He willingly volunteers to help others without expecting payment or reward.

A Scout is **FRIENDLY.** A Scout is a friend to all. He is a brother to other Scouts. He seeks to understand others. He respects those with ideas and customs that are different from his own.

A Scout is **COURTEOUS.** A Scout is polite to everyone regardless of age or position. He knows that good manners make it easier for people to get along together.

A Scout is **KIND.** A Scout understands there is strength in being gentle. He treats others as he wants to be treated. He does not harm or kill anything without reason.

A Scout is **OBEDIENT.** A Scout follows the rules of his family, school, and troop. He obeys the laws of his community and country. If he thinks these rules and laws are unfair, he tries to have them changed in an orderly manner rather than disobey them.

A Scout is **CHEERFUL.** A Scout looks for the bright side of life. He cheerfully does tasks that come his way. He tries to make others happy.

A Scout is **THRIFTY.** A Scout works to pay his way and to help others. He saves for the future. He protects and conserves natural resources. He carefully uses time and property.

A Scout is **BRAVE.** A Scout can face danger even if he is afraid. He has the courage to stand for what he thinks is right even if others laugh at him or threaten him.

A Scout is **CLEAN.** A Scout keeps his body and mind fit and clean. He goes around with those who believe in living by these same ideas. He helps keep his home and community clean.

A Scout is **REVERENT.** A Scout is reverent toward God. He is faithful in his religious duties. He respects the beliefs of others.

Demolition Derby Rules

Driver Regulations: All drivers MUST:

Be at least 16 years of age and have a driver's license.

Wear secured seat or safety belt and approved helmet.

Wear protective eyewear, shirt and full-length jeans. (No cutoffs.)

Furnish own automobile, with proof of ownership available upon request.

NOT extend arm outside of vehicle.

NOT be pregnant.

Racing Regulations:

Driver may maneuver forward or backward. NO DELIBERATE HITTING IN THE DRIVER'S DOOR. NO PULLING OF YOUR DOOR INTO THE PATH OF AN ONCOMING OPPONENT.

Driver MUST remain in car with helmet on and seat belt secured until the end of that race.

All cars must be removed from the grounds by noon of the day following the event.

All drivers MUST complete an Aggressive hit, with visible damage, on alternating competitors within the time limit announced at the drivers meeting. If a contact does not show visible results, YOU MAY BE DISQUALIFIED FOR SANDBAGGING. If your contacts do not vary equally between all of the participants on the track, YOU MAY BE DISQUALIFIED FOR TEAM DRIVING. IT IS EASILY DETECTED WHEN YOU ARE NOT COMPLYING. Absolutely NO pinning or holding competitor's vehicle.

Any driver that has two (2) fires, other than carburetor backfire, in the engine compartment OR one (1) fire in the passenger compartment shall be IMMEDIATELY DISQUALIFIED.

DIC Code of Standards for Cartoons

Storylines should enhance self esteem and cooperative behavior.

Avoid dangerous stunts that children could imitate.

Conflicts should be resolved using dialogue, negotiation, and meditation.

Antisocial behavior should not be portrayed as acceptable.

Violent behavior should only be shown when consequences
are realistically depicted.

Emily Post's Guidelines for Deportment When Having an Audience with the Pope

It is required that everybody be dressed in a sober and suitable manner.

Women must have their hair covered, must wear black or dark dresses with necklines that are not too low and skirts that are not too short.

Women may not have bare arms or legs.

No one may wear any but the most functional jewelry.

Men traditionally wear evening dress with tails or sack coat.

When the Pope appears on a portable throne carried by eight Swiss Guards, the audience rises.

When the Pope leaves the portable throne and sits in a fixed one, the audience may be seated.

When the Pope gives a benediction, the audience kneels.

The audience is over when the Pope mounts his portable throne and is carried out.

The Pope is addressed as "Your Holiness."

Cardinals, heads of state, ambassadors, or other important people may have a private audience.

In a special audience called a "baciomano," visitors stand in a single file around the room. When the Pope enters, they kneel and do not stand again until he leaves the room or makes a sign for them to rise. He passes from one visitor to another, extending his hand so that all may kiss his ring.

Non-Catholics must observe these guidelines with one exception: they need not make the sign of the cross.

eWorld's Standards for Living in an Electronic World

Rule #1. Everyone in eWorld is protected from harassment.

Rule #2. We only allow legal activities in eWorld.

Rule #3. We do our best to encourage safety and comfort, and discourage disruptive communication.

Rule #4. We encourage your participation in upholding eWorld Standards.

When in doubt about appropriate behavior in eWorld, remember that eWorld is an electronic world, but the people here are real. So, just as when you join any gathering of people, we ask that you treat others with respect and with care.

Father Flanagan's
Boys Town Axioms

There are no bad boys. There is only bad environment, bad training, bad example, bad thinking.

Keep them occupied, keep them busy; keep them playing on the football field, on the basketball court; keep them in our shops, our crafts, our hobby clubs. This is how you can develop good boys and girls and help eliminate so-called juvenile delinquency.

The whole family should unite in a community prayer each night to bring back God to the home and rebuild it as a spiritual unit of a hoped-for new world.

Work, rest and recreation are important the year round to get the most and the best out of the human side of life.

In the happiness brought to others, our own happiness is reflected.

There are no trivial people. There are only people with trivial thoughts and trivial interests.

Field & Stream's Tips
for Fly Fishing in Central Park

1. Ignore the people who give you funny looks.

2. Remember that a state fishing license is required and that state fishing regulations apply, but no permits are required.

3. All fishing is catch and release.

4. Avoid the weekends. That's when dogs chase Frisbees into the pond.

5. Watch where you cast. Remember, 20 million people visit the park annually, and most of them are not familiar with the back cast and wouldn't appreciate getting snagged by one of your flies.

6. Restrict your fishing to the daylight hours.

7. Acquire maps.

Film Extras: Guidelines from a Casting Coordinator

1. Arrive early for work. Make sure you park only in designated area.

2. Do not bring friends or relatives to work with you.

3. Please bring three changes of appropriate clothes, none of which are RED, SOLID BLACK, OR SOLID WHITE or having logos on them.

4. Do not wander off the set or leave holding area without notifying the appropriate person.

5. Food and beverages for extras are clearly designated. Do not consume items from the craft service table labeled "crew only."

6. Keep payment voucher on your person at all times. You will need to hand in this voucher once you are released.

7. Refrain from talking to working actors and crew members. Do not ask for autographs or take photographs.

8. Make sure your entire schedule is clear before accepting work. A film shoot day generally lasts 12–14 hours. PLEASE DO NOT ASK WHEN YOU WILL BE RELEASED. NO ONE KNOWS THE ANSWER TO THIS QUESTION.

9. Turn beepers off and leave mobile phones and mini-televisions in the holding area.

10. Do not change your appearance after you have been established on camera, unless you have been requested to by the wardrobe and hair/makeup departments.

11. Do not talk on set.

12. Do not bring valuables to work.

Freemasons: The Master Mason's Oath

Further, that I will acknowledge and obey all due signs and summonses sent to me from a Master Mason's Lodge, or given me by a brother of that Degree, if within the length of my cable tow.

Further, that I will always aid and assist all poor, distressed, worthy Master Masons, their widows and orphans, knowing them to be such, as far as their necessities may require, and my ability permit, without material injury to myself and family.

Further, that I will keep a worthy brother Master Mason's secrets inviolable, when communicated to and received by me as such, murder and treason excepted.

Further, that I will not aid, nor be present at, the initiation, passing, or raising of a woman, an old man in his dotage, a young man in his nonage, an atheist, a madman, or fool, knowing them to be such.

Further, that I will not sit in a Lodge of clandestine-made Masons, nor converse on the subject of Masonry with a clandestine-made Mason, nor one who has been expelled or suspended from a Lodge, while under that sentence, knowing him or them to be such.

Further, I will not cheat, wrong, nor defraud a Master Masons' Lodge, nor a brother of this Degree, knowingly, nor supplant him in any of his laudable undertakings, but will give him due and timely notice, that he may ward off all danger.

Further, that I will not knowingly strike a brother Master Mason, or otherwise do him personal violence in anger, except in the necessary defense of my family or property.

Further, that I will not have illegal carnal intercourse with a Master Mason's wife, his mother, sister, or daughter knowing them to be such, nor suffer the same to be done by others, if in my power to prevent.

Further, that I will not give the Grand Masonic word, in any other manner or form than that in which I shall receive it, and then in a low breath.

Further, that I will not give the Grand Hailing Sign of Distress except in case of the most imminent danger, in a just and lawful Lodge, or for the benefit of instruction; and if ever I should see it given, or hear the words accompanying it, by a worthy brother in distress, I will fly to his relief, if there is a greater probability of saving his life than losing my own.

The Fuller Brush Company: The Successful Man's Successful Habits of Work

1. Customer Courtesy

   a. Makes friends; plays hobbies and knows when to do so.

   b. Gives positive answers to excuses.

   c. Cares for adjustments properly; never hunts for defective goods.

   d. Handles no admissions and no sales tactfully.

2. Personal Qualities

   a. Personal appearance and manner.

b. The Fine and Dandy spirit.

c. Attitude toward the Company, toward product, toward himself.

d. Keeps studying and growing.

e. Puts one new idea into operation each day.

3. Good Business Methods

a. Works the law of averages, analyzes his work and builds his strength.

b. Is placed right in the territory and keeps territory record accurately.

c. Works territory right and does not scatter his efforts.

    d. Does not scatter future orders too far ahead.

    e. Builds good will and future business.

4. Time

    a. Puts in a full day's work.

    b. Makes profit producing number of dems.

    c. Places cards personally and sets early appointments.

    d. Makes evening calls frequently.

    e. Calls back on not-at-homes.

5. Outfit

    a. Knows his brushes and carries sufficient Handy Brushes.

    b. Carries the right brushes for the season.

    c. Case is neat and clean and changes samples frequently.

Gene Autry's Ten Cowboy Commandments

1. Do not take unfair advantage of an enemy.

2. Be a patriot.

3. Be gentle with children, elders and animals.

4. Do not possess racially or religiously intolerant ideas.

5. Don't drink or smoke.

6. Help people in distress.

7. Respect women, parents and your nation's laws.

8. Be a good worker.

9. Always tell the truth.

10. Never go back on your word.

General Colin Powell's Rules to Live By

1. It ain't as bad as you think. It will look better in the morning.

2. Get mad, then get over it.

3. Avoid having your ego so close to your position that when your position falls, your ego goes with it.

4. It can be done!

5. Be careful what you choose. You may get it.

6. Don't let adverse facts stand in the way of a good decision.

7. You can't make someone else's choices. You shouldn't let someone else make yours.

8. Check small things.

9. Share credit.

10. Remain calm. Be kind.

11. Have a vision.

12. Don't take counsel of your fears or naysayers.

13. Perpetual optimism is a force multiplier.

The General Services Administration Rules for Foreign Gifts to U.S. Government Employees

1. Refuse gifts of "more than minimal value."

2. Report and turn over the gifts you accept to their federal agency within 60 days.

3. If the agency doesn't want to keep the gift itself for display, it must report it to the GSA.

4. The GSA can give the gift to another federal agency that wants it for "official use."

5. If no federal agency wants it, the person who actually received it is given an opportunity to buy it at its appraised value.

6. If the recipient doesn't want it, GSA must offer it to state governments for display use only.

7. If none of the above wants the gift, and the state department concurs, it must be sold to the public by GSA's federal Supply Service. Gifts that either don't sell or have little or no commercial value can be destroyed.

Geneva Convention Rules of War

Rule 1: Warring nations cannot use chemical weapons against each other.

Rule 2: The use of expanding bullets or materials calculated to cause unnecessary suffering is prohibited.

Rule 3: The discharge of projectiles (such as bullets or rockets) from balloons is prohibited.

Rule 4: Prisoners of war must be humanely treated and protected from violence. Prisoners cannot be beaten or used for propaganda purposes (to try to change the way people think about something).

Rule 5: Prisoners of war must give their true name and rank, or they will lose their prisoner of war protection.

Rule 6: Nations must follow procedures to identify the dead and wounded and to send information to their families.

Rule 7: Killing anyone who has surrendered is prohibited.

Rule 8: Zones must be set up in fighting areas to which the sick and injured can be taken for treatment.

Rule 9: Special protection from attack is granted to civilian hospitals marked with the Red Cross.

Rule 10: The free passage of medical supplies is allowed.

Rule 11: Shipwrecked members of the armed forces at sea should be taken ashore to safety.

Rule 12: Any army that takes control of another country must provide food to the people in that country.

Rule 13: Attacks on civilians and undefended towns are prohibited.

Rule 14: Enemy submarines cannot sink merchant or business ships before passengers and crews have been saved.

Rule 15: A prisoner can be visited by a representative from his or her country, and they have the right to talk privately without observers.

Girl Scouts' Rules Regarding Cookie Sales

Local ordinances related to involvement of children in money-earning projects must be observed.

Each girl's participation must be voluntary.

The buddy system must be used.

A parent or other adult must know each girl's whereabouts when she is engaged in product sales.

Girls must be identifiable as Girl Scouts by wearing a membership pin or uniform or carrying a membership card.

Weather conditions must be suitable, and dress must be appropriate for those conditions.

Comfortable shoes and socks must be worn for long walks.

Girls must be familiar with the areas and neighborhoods in which they will sell.

Adults must accompany Brownie Girl Scouts.

Girls must participate in door-to-door sales only during daylight hours, unless accompanied by an adult.

Girls must learn and practice personal protection skills as outlined in their handbooks. For example:

- Do not enter the home of a stranger.

- Use safe pedestrian practices, especially when crossing at busy intersections.

- Do not carry large amounts of money. Provision for safeguarding the money must be made in advance.

The troop leader's or designated telephone number must be given for reorders or complaints; a girl must not give her telephone number.

The Golden Rule(s)

CHRISTIAN

All things whatsoever ye would that men should do to you, do ye even so to them; for this is the law and the prophets. (*Matthew 7:12*)

BRAHMAN

This is the sum of duty: Do naught unto others which would cause you pain if done to you . (*Mahabharata 5:1517*)

BUDDHIST

Hurt not others in ways that you yourself would find hurtful. (*Udana-Varga 5:18*)

CONFUCIAN

Surely it is the maxim of loving-kindness: Do not unto others what you would not have done unto you. (*Analects 15:23*)

TAOIST

Regard your neighbor's gain as your own gain and your neighbor's loss as your own loss. (*T'ai Shang Kan Ying P'ien*)

ZOROASTRIAN

That nature alone is good which refrains from doing unto another whatsoever is not good for itself. (*Dadistan-i-dinik 94:5*)

JEWISH

What is hateful to you, do not to your fellow man. That is the entire Law; all the rest is commentary. (*Talmud, Shabbat 31a*)

ISLAMIC

No one of you is a believer until he desires for his brother that which he desires for himself. (*Sunnah*)

Graduation Requirements for the Scottsdale Unified School District

Write and speak effectively. Speak articulately and listen attentively.

Think critically and reason logically.

Demonstrate creative expression.

Demonstrate the ability to compute, reason and communicate mathematically.

Understand the structure, operation and relationships in the United States.

Conduct valid research. Demonstrate the ability to identify and solve problems. Use technology effectively.

Demonstrate the ability to analyze critical issues.

Demonstrate an awareness of other cultures.

Demonstrate a knowledge of career opportunities.

Demonstrate skills necessary for independent living.

Demonstrate personal and community responsibility.

A Guide for the Polite Panhandler

1. Try to make eye contact, recognizing the humanity of the panhandled.

2. Always say "please" and "thank you."

3. Never follow or yell at people; harassment is illegal.

4. Do not block the sidewalk or interfere with commercial businesses.

5. Offering to work for food is frequently effective.

6. Smile—you can catch more flies with honey than with vinegar.

7. Never use profane language.

8. Remember, everyone has the right to say no.

9. Beggars are the moral stoplights of society; your presence and actions should make passersby question the relationship between their moral or religious values and current socio-economic practices and policies.

Harley-Davidson's Rules for Safety

When enjoying your Harley-Davidson motorcycle, be sure to ride safely and within the limits of the law and your abilities.

Ride with your headlights on and watch out for the other person.

Always wear a helmet, proper eyewear and appropriate clothing and insist that your passenger does, too.

Never ride under the influence of alcohol or drugs.

Know your own Harley and read and understand your owner's manual from cover to cover.

Protect your right to ride by joining the American Motorcyclist Association.

. . . And the Legend Rolls On.

La Cosa Nostra Oath of *Omerta*

Never break the vow of silence.

Never talk to any outsider about the existence of La Cosa Nostra.

Never become an informant.

Never covet the wife or girlfriend of another made guy or his daughter
if your intentions are dishonorable.

Never do anything against the best interests of the organization.

Lands' End Principles of Doing Business

Principle 1. We do everything we can to make our products better.

Principle 2. We price our products fairly and honestly.

Principle 3. We accept any return, for any reason, at any time. Guaranteed. Period.

Principle 4. We ship faster than anyone we know of.

Principle 5. We believe that what is best for our customer is best for all of us.

Principle 6. We are able to sell at lower prices because we have eliminated middlemen; because we don't buy branded merchandise with high protected markups; and because we have placed our contracts with manufacturers who have proved that they are cost-conscious and efficient.

Principle 7. We are able to sell at lower prices because we operate efficiently. Our people are hard working, intelligent and share in the success of the company.

Principle 8. We are able to sell at lower prices because we support no fancy emporiums with their high overhead. Our main location is in the middle of a 40-acre cornfield in rural Wisconsin.

A Library Code of Conduct

No abusive language.

No animals.

No bare feet.

No candy.

No disruptive behavior.

No disturbing noise.

No distribution of materials.

No feet on furniture.

No food or drink.

No playing of games.

No running.

No sleeping.

No smoking.

No soliciting.

No sports equipment.

Mary Kay Cosmetics Core Values

Do unto others as you would have them do unto you.

God first, family second and career third.

The more you give into the lives of others, the more will come back into your own. Help others get what they want, and you will get what you want.

Make others feel important.

Praise people to success. Sandwich every piece of criticism between two layers of praise.

Enthusiasm bypasses the conscious mind.

The speed of the leader is the speed of the gang.

The Miller Brewing Company's Guidelines for Responsible Drinking

Pace yourself.

Plan your drinking.

Pick a partner.

Take time to rest before leaving.

MIT Guide to Lock Picking

1. Apply a sheer force.

2. Find the pin that is binding the most.

3. Push that pin up until you feel it set at the sheer line.

4. Go to step 2.

Moltar's Oven-Cleaning Tips

1. Allocate at least eight hours to your task.

2. Iron ore from sector 24 of the planet Cyclo is helpful in removing ugly residue build-up.

3. If you must use commercial products, do not inhale fumes (Earth only).

4. There's no substitute for good old-fashioned elbow grease.

5. Two words: adequate ventilation. Happy cleaning!

Monopoly® Rules Regarding Jail

A player lands in jail (1) if his piece lands on space marked Go To Jail, (2) if he draws a card marked Go to Jail, (3) if he throws doubles three times in succession.

When a player is sent to jail, he cannot collect $200 salary in that move.

New York City Transit Authority Subway Rules

Please Do Not:

Destroy subway property.

Litter.

Graffiti.

Drink alcoholic beverages.

Panhandle or beg.

Use amplification devices on platforms.

Use more than one seat per person.

Block free movement.

Lie down.

Engage in unauthorized commercial activities.

Enter tracks, tunnels and non-public areas.

Transport bulky items likely to inconvenience others.

Play a radio audible to others.

Create an unsanitary condition (spit, urinate).

Engage in an activity that creates a hazard (roller blading, skateboarding).

Carry an open beverage onto a subway or bus.

New York Marathon Last-Minute Tips from the Psyching Team

1. Don't worry about worrying.

2. Say all your fears out loud.

3. Go over all pre-race and race details in your head.

4. Body scan.

5. Decide what to wear in advance.

6. Imagine yourself having a great run.

7. Plan to take music breaks during the race.

8. Do some relaxation exercises.

9. Plan to affirm yourself during the race.

10. Enjoy fellow runners' company during the race.

New York State's Rules for Divorce Lawyers

1. Divorce lawyers are banned from having sex with their clients.

2. They are banned from demanding a nonrefundable retainer.

3. They are banned from foreclosing on their client's mortgage to get paid.

4. Lawyers no longer have to advise a client how to file a grievance against them.

NFL's Media Interview Do's and Don'ts

INTERVIEW DO'S

1. Be prepared.

2. Be positive.

3. Praise your teammates.

4. Talk in sound bites.

5. Smile.

6. Be enthusiastic.

7. Be personable.

8. Be available and cooperative.

9. Be polite in difficult situations.

10. Bridge to your message.

INTERVIEW DON'TS

1. Don't say "No comment."

2. Don't talk about money.

3. Don't be negative.

4. Don't hide.

5. Don't lose your cool.

6. Don't forget the fishbowl.

7. Don't be sarcastic.

8. Don't use fillers.

9. Don't cop an attitude.

10. Don't miss the opportunity.

Nintendo Video Game Content Guidelines

No random, gratuitous, and/or excessive violence.

No subliminal or overt political messages.

No domestic violence and/or abuse.

No ethnic, racial, religious, nationalistic, or sexual stereotypes of languages.

No use of illegal drugs, smoking materials, alcohol.

No graphic illustration of death.

No sexually suggestive or explicit content.

No excessive force in sports games.

No profanity or obscenity.

No sexist language or depictions.

NRA Member's Mission

In service to the law-abiding American public, the National Rifle Association seeks to:

Protect and defend the Constitution of the United States, especially the Second Amendment right of the individual to keep and bear arms.

Train citizens in marksmanship and in the safe handling and efficient use of firearms.

Foster and promote the shooting sports on all levels.

Support crime-fighting measures, such as mandatory sentencing, probation/parole reform, adequate prison space and properly equipped law enforcement.

Promote public safety, law and order and the national defense.

Provide training for law enforcement agencies in marksmanship and firearms handling.

Promote hunter safety, resource conservation and proper wildlife management.

Procter & Gamble's Helpful Hints for Dishwashing

Scoop away food particles from items to be washed.

Remove grease from pots, pans, skillets before washing.

Soak heavily soiled pans and utensils before washing.

Wash out coffeepots and teapots after use. Rinse thoroughly.

Wipe the sink and counter tops with a detergent solution.

A Reporter's Tips for Dealing with the Press in a Crisis

Don't lie.

Don't stonewall.

Never say "No comment." But don't be afraid to say "I don't know."

Don't be dominated by lawyers. They hoard information for the courtroom.

Be accessible.

Accommodate the media. Make it physically easier for them to work.

Above all, remember this: You can't stop the reporting of a story. You can only influence it.

Ritz-Carlton Three Steps of Service

1. A warm and sincere greeting. Use the guest name, if and when possible.

2. Anticipation and compliance with guest needs.

3. Fond farewell. Give them a warm good-bye and use their names, if and when possible.

"We are ladies and gentlemen serving ladies and gentlemen."

Satchel Paige's Rules of Life

1. Avoid fried meats which angry up the blood.

2. If your stomach disputes you, lie down and pacify it with cool thoughts.

3. Keep the juices flowing by jangling around gently as you move.

4. Go very light on the vices such as carrying on in society; the social ramble ain't restful.

5. Avoid running at all times.

6. Don't look back; something might be gaining on you.

Sixth-Grade Science Class
Safety and Conduct Rules

1. No hats.

2. No gum, food, drinks.

3. Always be prepared with pen/pencil.

4. No rushing or running.

5. No disrespect toward any person, project, or effort.

6. Listen to all directions completely and carefully.

7. Follow instructions carefully.

8. Be creative and safe.

9. Be cooperative and considerate.

10. Don't be afraid to ask yourself or your partner "What if I. . . ."

11. Report any broken glass to the teacher immediately.

12. Report any injuries to your teacher immediately.

13. If it is not yours, don't touch it.

14. Be extremely careful when using sharp objects.

15. Dry any spills with a sponge first, then with a paper towel.

16. Always return equipment/supplies where they belong.

17. Always clean up after yourself.

18. Never do anything to endanger anyone else.

19. When using fire:

   a. Do not wear loose clothing.

   b. Pull hair back away from flame.

c. Keep paper away from flame.

d. Know where the fire extinguisher and the fire blanket are.

e. Know how to use the fire extinguisher and the fire blanket.

f. Report any mishap to the teacher immediately.

g. Use proper sense and common sense in all decisions.

h. During any incident, stay cool! Never panic!

20. When using water, designate a desk for water, and another area for notes.

Smith System Rules of Driving

1. Drive defensively.

2. Always leave yourself an out.

3. Get the big picture.

4. Aim high in steering.

Smokey the Bear's Junior Forest Rangers' Easy Rules for Preventing Forest Fires

Remind your parents and friends to:

Break matches in two. When they can hold the burned end between their fingers, no fire is left.

Crush out smokes; then use the ashtray.

Drown campfires; then stir the ashes to make sure they are out.

Never burn grass, brush, or trash on windy days. When they do burn it, they should have plenty of help.

The Stew Leonard's Philosophy

SATISFY . . . FILL OUR CUSTOMER'S NEED!

Rule #1–The customer is always right.

Rule #2–If the customer is wrong, go back and reread Rule 1.

We believe in bending over backwards to give our customers a better deal because we know that only happy customers come back.

We believe that a customer who complains is our best friend because she cares enough to give us the opportunity to improve.

TEAMWORK

We believe that our greatest asset is not on our company's financial statement–it's our team of people.

We believe in helping our people succeed–to become themselves at their very best.

You can't have a great company without first starting with great people.

We believe in growing our own and promoting from within. That's why we're always training somebody to do our job—so we are available for promotion.

EXCELLENCE

Our goal is to be the best food store in the country, not the biggest.

We believe that the only place that price comes before quality is in the dictionary.

We believe that low price alone brings shoppers, but quality brings customers.

WOW! DON'T FAIL TO PROMOTE!

We believe in making our customers say wow!

We believe in showmanship. If we fail to promote, a terrible thing will happen—nothing!

We believe in making Stew Leonard's a fun place to shop and work—a happy place filled with smiles, because if we're happy and having fun, chances are our customers will be too.

The Ten Commandments

You shall have no other gods before me.

You shall not make yourself a graven image.

You shall not take the name of the Lord your God in vain.

Remember the Sabbath day, to keep it holy.

Honor your father and your mother.

You shall not kill.

You shall not commit adultery.

You shall not steal.

You shall not bear false witness against your neighbor.

You shall not covet your neighbor's house; you shall not covet your neighbor's wife, or his manservant, or his maidservant, or his ox, or his ass, or anything that is your neighbor's.

The Ten LEGO Characteristics

unlimited play potential

for girls, for boys

fun for every age

year-round play

stimulating and motivated play

long hours of play

development, imagination, creativity

the more LEGO elements, the greater the value

always up-to-the-minute

safety and quality

Tips for Teens: Ten Commandments of Good Conduct

1. Be a teen with taste, dressing appropriately for the occasion.

2. Act like a lady and he will treat you as such.

3. Be able to enjoy an everyday date as well as the glamour occasions.

4. Don't hang on him too possessively.

5. Don't have him fetch and carry just to create an impression.

6. Make up if you like but do not try to make over what you are.

7. Be popular with girls as well as boys.

8. Learn to like sports—it's an all-American topic in which boys are interested.

9. Don't be too self-sufficient; boys like to feel needed.

10. Be natural.

United Nations Convention on the Rights of a Child

1. Every child has a right to life.

2. Every child has a right to a name at birth and a nationality.

3. Every child has the right to live with his or her parent unless it is against the child's best interests.

4. Special protection shall be given to refugee children.

5. Every child has the right to the highest standard of health and medical care possible.

6. The child has a right to education. The state is to ensure that primary education is free and compulsory.

7. No child shall be subjected to torture, cruel treatment, unlawful arrest, or deprivation of liberty.

8. Children under 15 shall not be recruited into the armed forces.

United States Senate Pages' Code of Conduct

A Page's conduct must always reflect honorably on the U.S. Congress.

Acts of disrespect or disobedience to any staff, the Director or any Capitol Police Officer are prohibited.

A Page is free to express him/herself in any responsible manner. Behavior that infringes on the privacy of others or is disruptive is prohibited.

It is expected that public displays of affection between Pages will not take place during Page Program functions out of respect for the rights of others.

Vulgar acts or gestures by the Pages in verbal or written form are prohibited, as is the drawing of vulgar pictures or caricatures on government property.

A Page is prohibited from lying or any other form of deceptive or misleading behavior.

Intentional destruction, damage or defacement of property (including graffiti) is prohibited.

Physically injuring another person, whether the injury is by intent or incidental to conduct otherwise in violation of the Code, is prohibited.

Threat of force or intimidation is prohibited.

The Page Residence Hall is part of the larger community, and Pages should be aware that they enjoy no special status in that community. Pages obey District of Columbia and Federal laws, including drug law. Neither the Residence Hall staff nor the Doorkeeper can or will protect the Pages from the consequences of violations of the law. Pages are fully responsible for their own conduct.

A guest of the opposite sex of the host/hostess Page may _not_ stay overnight in the room of the host/hostess.

University of Pittsburgh's Center for Medical Ethics' Guide to Organ Procurement

1. Patients must be dead before the organs are taken.

2. Although patients may be allowed to die under certain circumstances, they must never actively be killed.

3. Patient or family consent must precede organ retrieval.

War and Navy Departments'
Guide to Great Britain for the Enlisted Man

No time to fight old wars.   You may think of the English as enemy Redcoats who fought against us in the American Revolution and the War of 1812. But there is no time today to fight old wars over again or bring up old grievances.

Don't be a show off.   The British dislike bragging and showing off. American wages and American soldier's pay are the highest in the world. The British "Tommy" is apt to be specially touchy about the difference between his wages and yours.

Remember there's a war on.   Britain may look a little shop-worn and grimy to you. The British people are anxious for you to know that in normal times Britain looks much prettier, cleaner, neater. . . . If British civilians look dowdy and badly dressed, it is not because they do not like good clothes or know how to wear them. All clothing is rationed and the British know that they help war production by wearing an old suit or dress until it cannot be patched any longer. Old clothes are good form. If you are invited into a British home and the host exhorts you to "eat up–

there's plenty on the table," go easy. It may be the family's rations for a whole week spread out to show their hospitality.

Remember that the British are like the Americans in many ways— but not in all ways. They will like your frankness as long as it is friendly. They will expect you to be generous. They are not given to back-slapping and they are shy about showing their affections. . . . Two actions on your part will slow up the friendship between yourself and the British soldier: swiping his girl, and not appreciating what his army has been up against. Yes, and rubbing it in that you are better paid than he is! And you don't have to tell the British about lend-lease food. They know about it and appreciate it.

Keep out of arguments. You can rub a Britisher the wrong way by telling him "we came over and won the last one." Use your head before you sound off, and remember how long the British alone held Hitler off without any help from anyone.

In a nutshell: Don't make fun of British speech or accents. You sound just as funny to them, but they will be too polite to show it.

Avoid comments on the British Government or politics. Don't try to tell the British that America won the last war or make wisecracks about the war debts or about British defeats in this war.

NEVER criticize the King or the Queen.

Don't criticize the food, beer, or cigarettes to the British. Remember they have been at war since 1939.

Use common sense on all occasions.

It is always impolite to criticize your host; it is militarily stupid to criticize your allies.

(circa 1942)

West Point Cadet's Rules of Closet Order

WARDROBE

Hat Display:
White Hat, Gray Hat, Tar Bucket, Plume.

From Left to Right:
Full Dress, India Whites (in season), Dress Gray, Blazer, Gray Jacket, Class Shirts, White Shirts (in season), BDUs, Civilian Clothes (1st Class only).

Footgear:
(Heels against the wall) Over Shoes, Shower Shoes, Slippers.

NOTE: Skirts and trousers may be hung under their respective jackets.

COAT CLOSET

Items will be arranged from left to right in the following order:
Cadet Raincoat, Black Overcoat, Dress Mess (women only), Long Overcoat, Short

Overcoat, Parka, BDU Jacket, Civilian Coat (First Class Only), Bathrobe, Beachrobe.

Footgear:
Civilian Shoes (First Class Only).

NOTE: Bathrobes and parkas from other Service Academies will directly follow the USMA counterpart.

One pair of pajamas being worn may be stored/folded on the hanger bar under the beachrobe.

The Young Man's Training
for an Effective Life

A young man ought to be a clean, wholesome, vigorous animal.

Do not condescend to the ordinary barbaric vices. One must avoid drunkenness, gluttony, licentiousness, and getting into dirt of any kind.

You need a strong mental grip, a wholesome capacity for hard work.

Live with honor, on honor.

Some things that an honorable man cannot do, never does:

- He never wrongs or degrades a woman.

- He never oppresses or cheats a person weaker or poorer than himself.

- He never betrays a trust.

- He is honest, sincere, candid, and generous.

(circa 1912)

Acknowledgments

Special thanks for their help and contributions: Shirley Sykes, Alcoholics Anonymous World Services; Brian Michael Kelly; Karen Kovack, Antioch University; John Melingagio, Boys Town; Leonard Pease, National Demolition Derby Association; Daria Dionta, *Field & Stream*; Phil Shook; Owen Rice and Kim Petrosky, Casting Coordinators; Stephanie Leuenberger, The Fuller Brush Company; Dee Wruble, Lands' End; Marge Ping, The Miller Brewing Company; Leslie Hammond, National Football League; Paul Roa, The Ritz-Carlton, New York; Jill Leonard, Stew Leonard's; Robert Benoit, U.S. Senate Sergeant at Arms. And extra special, super deluxe thanks to all-star Robin Dellabough, for the research and major legwork; Peter Strupp for the avid off-duty ferreting; and Megan O'Connor for the early enthusiasm and initial legwork.

Credits

"Alcoholics Anonymous: The Twelve Steps." "The Twelve Steps" are reprinted with permission of Alcoholics Anonymous World Services, Inc. Permission to reprint this material does not mean that A.A. has reviewed or approved the contents of this publication, nor that A.A. agrees with the views expressed herein. A.A. is a program of recovery from alcoholism only—use of the Twelve Steps in connection with programs and activities which are patterned after A.A., but which address other problems, does not imply otherwise.

"The American Kennel Club Guidelines for Dog Show Judges." Excerpt from "Guidelines for Conformation Dog Show Judges," American Kennel Club, Inc.

"Anthony Robbins' Five Rules for Walking on Hot Coals." From Anthony Robbins' "Unleash the Power Within" seminar, as reported in "Mr. President: Cool Moss," an op-ed piece in *The Wall Street Journal,* January 25, 1995.

"Antioch University Sexual Offense Policy: Consent." Excerpt from the University's Sexual Consent Policy, established 1991.

"Arthur Elgort's *Models Manual.*" Excerpt courtesy of Arthur Elgort Ltd.

"Attaining Super-Health: A Few Hints from Superman." From *Superman Archives,* circa 1938.

"Avon's Principles." David H. McConnell, Avon's Founder, circa 1898.

"Baltasar Gracián's *Oraculo Manual.*" Excerpt, circa 1650.

"Boy Scout Laws." Boy Scouts of America.

"Demolition Derby Rules." Excerpt, *National Demolition Derby Association Uniform Rules and Regulations.*

"DIC Code of Standards for Cartoons." DIC produces animated films and video games, including "Sonic the Hedgehog" and others.

"Emily Post's Guidelines for Deportment When Having an Audience with the Pope." Adapted from *Emily Post's Etiquette,* 12th edition, pages 153–5. Funk and Wagnalls, Ramsey, New Jersey.

"eWorld's Standards for Living in an Electronic World." Excerpts from eWorld's guidelines for appropriate online behavior.

"Father Flanagan's Boys Town Axioms." Father Edward J. Flanagan, Founder, Boys Town. Courtesy of Father Flanagan's Boys' Home, Boys Town, Nebraska.

"*Field & Stream*'s Tips for Fly Fishing in Central Park." From Phil Shook's "Angling in the Big Apple," *Field & Stream,* April 1994, page 74.

"Film Extras: Guidelines from a Casting Coordinator." Courtesy of Owen Rice and Kim Petrosky, Chicago-area casting coordinators.

"Freemasons: The Master Mason's Oath." Excerpts from *Handbook of Secret Organizations,* William J. Whalen. The Bruce Publishing Company, Milwaukee, Wisconsin, 1966.

"The Fuller Brush Company: The Successful Man's Successful Habits of Work." From early sales personnel guidelines, courtesy of The Fuller Brush Company.

"Gene Autry's Ten Cowboy Commandments." Circa 1930.

"General Colin Powell's Rules to Live By." From various speeches, reported in multiple news publications.

"The General Services Administration Rules for Foreign Gifts to U.S. Government Employees." Excerpted from *Title IV*, U.S. Code.

"Geneva Convention Rules of War." From the 1864 Geneva Convention treaty regarding international rules of war.

"Girl Scouts' Rules Regarding Cookie Sales." Girl Scouts of the USA.

"Graduation Requirements for the Scottsdale Unified School District." Scottsdale Unified School District, Scottsdale, Arizona.

"A Guide for the Polite Panhandler." From a publication of the City Advocates in Solidarity with the Homeless, Baltimore, Maryland.

"Harley-Davidson's Rules for Safety." Courtesy of Harley-Davidson, Inc.

"La Cosa Nostra Oath of *Omerta*." Translated from FBI surveillance tapes of an induction ceremony in Providence, Rhode Island.

"Lands' End Principles of Doing Business" [Excerpts]. Lands' End, 1992.

"A Library Code of Conduct." Westchester County, New York, Library System.

"Mary Kay Cosmetics Core Values." Courtesy of Gwyn Hoyt, Senior Sales Director, Mary Kay Cosmetics.

"The Miller Brewing Company's Guidelines for Responsible Drinking." Excerpt from "Let's Talk Over a Beer," a Miller Brewing Company publication on responsible drinking.

"MIT Guide to Lock Picking." Copyright 1987, 1991, Theodore T. Tool (Ted the Tool). All rights reserved.

"Moltar's Oven-Cleaning Tips." Cartoon Network's "Space Ghost Coast to Coast" is directed by Moltar of the Molten Planet, who is a renowned expert on oven maintenance. Tips posted on the Cartoon Network's area on America Online. Keyword: Kids.

"Monopoly® Rules Regarding Jail." Monopoly®, the distinctive design of the game board, as well as each of the distinctive elements of the board and the playing pieces are trademarks of Tonka Corporation for its real estate trading game and game equipment. © 1935, 1946, 1961, 1985, 1994 Parker Brothers, a Division of Tonka Corporation, Beverly, Massachusetts, 01915.

"New York City Transit Authority Subway Rules." From the Transit Authority's publicly posted riders' rules.

"New York Marathon Last-Minute Tips from the Psyching Team." From "New York City Marathon Final Instructions," distributed by the New York Road Runners Club.

"New York State's Rules for Divorce Lawyers." Professional guidelines.

"NFL's Media Interview Do's and Don'ts." The National Football League's "Media Relations Playbook."

"Nintendo Video Game Content Guidelines." Excerpts from Nintendo's Parents' Informational Brochure, 1993.

"NRA Member's Mission." National Rifle Association.

"Procter & Gamble's Helpful Hints for Dishwashing." Excerpt from early product promotional material.

"A Reporter's Tips for Dealing with the Press in a Crisis." John Holusha, *The New York Times,* as reported in the *Stanford Business School Magazine,* June 1994.

"Ritz-Carlton Three Steps of Service." From the Ritz-Carlton Credo Card, which is carried by all Ritz-Carlton employees at all times.

"Satchel Paige's Rules of Life." Robert LeRoy (Satchel) Paige, 1906–1982.

"Sixth-Grade Science Class Safety and Conduct Rules." Irvington Middle School. Irvington, New York.

"Smith System Rules of Driving." Adapted from the driver-training film, *The Smith Driving System.*

"Smokey the Bear's Junior Forest Rangers' Easy Rules for Preventing Forest Fires." From U.S. Forest Service promotional material, circa 1955.

"The Stew Leonard's Philosophy." Courtesy of Stew Leonard's University.

"The Ten Commandments." Exodus 20:3-17, the Bible.

"The Ten LEGO Characteristics." Courtesy of LEGO Systems Inc.

"*Tips for Teens:* Ten Commandments of Good Conduct." From *Tips for Teens,* Benjamin Darling, page 37, Chronicle Books, San Francisco, California.

"United Nations Convention on the Rights of a Child." Excerpts from the 41 articles of rights adopted by the United Nations in 1989.

"United States Senate Pages' Code of Conduct." Excerpts from the *Congressional Research Service Report for Congress*, September 27, 1990, pages CRS44–47.

"University of Pittsburgh's Center for Medical Ethics' Guide to Organ Procurement." From the "Dead Donor Rule," a paper by Robert M. Arnold of the University of Pittsburgh's Center for Medical Ethics which was published in the June 1992 issue of the *Kennedy Institute of Ethics Journal*.

"War and Navy Departments' Guide to Great Britain for the Enlisted Man." Excerpts from "A Short Guide to Great Britain," published and distributed by the U.S. War and Navy Departments to prepare enlisted men for their wartime journeys abroad, circa 1942.

"West Point Cadet's Rules of Closet Order." From *USCC Reg 701-1*, pp. B-3, B-5, C-3.

"The Young Man's Training for an Effective Life." Excerpts from *The Training for an Effective Life* by Charles W. Eliot, President of Harvard University, published by Houghton Mifflin Company, 1915.